Dedication

This work is dedicated to Anne Kerrigan, Derek Gunn, Chris Pittman and Kristen Good. All of you brought the Bridgewater Triangle alive for me. I thank you for that.

Table of Contents

Dighton Rock State Park

Freetown – Fall River State Forest

The Red Headed Hitchhiker

The Rehoboth Village Cemetery

Shad Factory Mill/Pond

Anawan Rock

Horbine School

Taunton State Hospital

Mount Pleasant Cemetery

Paul A. Dever/Camp Miles Standish

Mayflower Hill Cemetery: The Grave of Pearl E. French

Lake Nippenicket

Hockomock Swamp

Tillinghast Hall, Bridgewater State University

Preface

You may be wondering just who I am to put together a tour book highlighting a few of the controversial spots in the Bridgewater Triangle. I've been asking myself the same question and here's my conclusion. I've lived in the area most of my life perhaps, just like many of you. I've explored the Bridgewater Triangle just like you. The Bridgewater Triangle has intrigued me just like you.

For a brief year I ran the Bay State Paranormal Center. I learned a lot through that experience and a few of the experiences really drove me away from most things paranormal for a while. However, you know how it is, something about the paranormal always pulls you back in. Next thing I know, I'm driving around to all the old spots and taking another look, another listen and now there's a tour book for you to do the same.

And also like many of you, I've had a lifelong fascination with the paranormal. At times, it dared not speak its name it scared me so much but over time I came to see that it wasn't so much the boogey man under my bed but a part of my natural surroundings. Isn't that what the Bridgewater Triangle is, part of our natural surroundings? As such, explore it with vigor, an open mind and the utmost respect.

Respect brings me to a strong suggestion I want to leave you with. Please respect the locations you visit. Keep in mind that there may be people living in or around the area, that the location may have sentimental or financial value and leave it as you found it. Preserve it for your children's children.

Dighton Rock State Park

Location:
Bay View Avenue, Dighton, Massachusetts

GPS Information:
N 41°48.711', W071°06.560'

Site Information:
This park closes at 5pm. The building is not open every day. Check before going out to see the rock as the schedule can change.

Lore:
The rock itself has inscriptions of unknown origins that have been attributed to the Knights Templar, Vikings and/or Native Americans.

Freetown – Fall River State Forest

Location:
Slab Ridge Road, Freetown, Massachusetts – although there are several other park entry points

GPS Information:
N 41°46.754', W071°02.523'

Site Information:
The park closes thirty minutes after sundown. Be thoughtful about what trails you drive your vehicle through as the dense foliage will scratch your paint job and there are some roads that can be difficult to impassable due to pooling rain water and rocks.

Lore:
While Profile Rock may be the most prolific location, there have been various types of unexplained supernatural occurrences within the confines of this park. Satanic cults, heart breaking murders, puckwudgies and the ghost of King Phillip have all been spotted here.

The Red Headed Hitchhiker

Location: Town line signs on route 44; going west passing from Dighton to Rehoboth and going east passing from Swansea to Rehoboth

GPS Information:
Westerly direction: N 41°52.178', W071°12.079';
Easterly direction: N 41°50.012', W071°17.747'; sign may be obscured by foliage

Lore:
If you pull up to one of the Rehoboth town line signs, beep three times and then continue on your way into Rehoboth. You might possibly look into your rearview mirror and see the Red Headed Hitchhiker sitting in your backseat. He is most likely to visit you on a dark evening when you're driving alone.

The Red Headed Hitchhiker has a head full of red hair, a red beard and wears a red flannel shirt with a pair of jeans. He's been seen walking along the dark and woody stretch of route 44 and sometimes standing outside of a stopped car window. Perhaps you've driven past him without realizing that you've past a specter on the prowl. No one knows who he was when he was amongst the living. If you're lucky enough to share his company maybe you can find out.

The Rehoboth Village Cemetery

Location: Bay State Road, Rehoboth, Massachusetts, almost directly off of route 44

GPS Information
N 41°50.458', W071°15.556'

Lore:
Two sisters researching their family genealogy observed a man visiting a grave. They believed him to be in prayer alternating between sobbing, laughing and muttering to himself. During the ten minutes they watched this man they noticed that he was not clothed in modern dress, he had more of a dated look. Once he noticed that the sisters were watching him he began yelling at them. They became concerned thinking he may be dangerous and then he simply vanished.

Shad Factory Mill/Pond

Location:
Reed Street, Rehoboth, Massachusetts

GPS Information
N 41°48.529', W071°16.701'

Site Information:
This area now serves as a fish ladder.

Lore:
A man clothed in dark garments appears and vanishes and behaves in a menacing manner. Others report an old man standing by the ruins of the mill and scaring them off.

Anawan Rock

Location: Winthrop Street, Rehoboth, Massachusetts, Route 44. On the left if going west and on the right if coming east.

GPS Information:
N 41°51.952', W071°12.874'

Site Information: Very easy to drive by and miss. Look for a small metal sign saying, "Anawan Rock" near the road. It's easy to park off the street and the rock is down a bending, gravelly path.

Lore:
The story begins with the capture of King Phillip's uncle, Chief Anawan by Captain Benjamin Church on August 28, 1676. Since then people have seen dancing lights, have heard drums and what many think is a Native American voice yelling, "Stand and fight!"

Horbine School

Location:
Not provided, Rehoboth, Massachusetts

GPS Information:
Not provided

Site Information:
Once a year, teachers and students dress in period costumes and conduct class in the old fashioned school. Largely due to the report given below many have come to visit the school and often vandalize it when they do. This has resulted in unfortunate mounting expenses for the Historical Society. There are skeletons in the attic at this school but they belong to birds and are not there as the result of something dark and sinister.

Lore:
An older woman went to the window of the school and observed class in session. She saw children and a teacher in old fashioned clothing. The teacher gave her an aggravated look and the woman left.

Taunton State Hospital

Location:
At the end of the street, 60 Hodges Street, Taunton, Massachusetts

GPS Information:
N 41°54.822', W071°06.116'

Site Information:
This is a facility owned and run by the Commonwealth of Massachusetts. There are minors housed at these facilities. Built in 1854 and known as the State Lunatic Hospital at Taunton, the original hospital was torn down in 2009. This location has many additional buildings with their own spooky stories.

Lore:
Along with the insane, promiscuous young women were often interred here by their families. Stories including satanic rituals, a shadow man, screams and cold spots are just a taste of what has been experienced on these hospital grounds.

Mount Pleasant Cemetery

Location:
The intersection of W. Weir Street and Cohannet Street, Taunton, Massachusetts

GPS Information:
N 41°53.648', W071°06.055'

Lore:
It's not so much this cemetery as it is this area of Taunton. It's part of a mini-triangle in Taunton within the Bridgewater Triangle of which the cemetery serves as one vertex. It extends down Winthrop Street to Highland Street, from Highland Street to Cohannet Street.

The author (me) lived in two homes on Winthrop Street and had multiple paranormal experiences in both locations. When I was running the Bay State Paranormal Center, a surprising number of calls were logged from residents in this area detailing incidents of a paranormal nature. The location of this area is on route 44 in Taunton which is where many other haunted locations are found.

In this cemetery is laid to rest the body of an original owner of the first home I occupied in the area. I believe that I had a direct experience with this person in that home. He loved the house as much and likely more than I did He was a prominent citizen in Taunton and the Commonwealth of Massachusetts. According to Southcoast Ghost there are many notable figures now resting in this cemetery. If you visit, appreciate the beauty of the grounds and please do not disrespect the sanctity of this eternal resting place.

Paul A. Dever School /Camp Miles Standish

Location:
1380 Bay Street, Taunton, Massachusetts

GPS Information:
N 41°56.763', W071°06.937'

Site Information:
Initially serving the World War II effort, it readied soldiers to be sent to the European theater of war and then served as a prisoner of war camp to captured Italian and German soldiers. After the war, it eventually became a school and home for mentally disabled people. It is owned by the Commonwealth of Massachusetts and is patrolled diligently.

Lore:
The incidents are almost too numerous to list and consist of light specters, cries for help, glowing apparitions and banging/knocking noises.

Mayflower Hill Cemetery: The Grave of Pearl E. French

Location:
Broadway, Taunton, Massachusetts. Entrance is squarely between E. Britannia Street and Washington Street.

GPS Information:
N 41°55.242', W071°15.364'

Lore:
The rumor is that young Pearl French died tragically in a house fire when she was but four years old. Her grandparents were so grief stricken that they had fashioned a rocking chair monument at her grave. In reality, she died from Spinal Meningitis as did her cousin, Veva Johnson, who was laid to rest beside her. No matter the cause of Pearl's death, she has been seen early morning walkers; Mayflower Hill Cemetery is popular with those serious about walking for fitness and Pearl has been spotted many times by these very same walkers.

Lake Nippenicket, "Lake Nip"

Location: Pleasant Street, Route 104, Bridgewater, Massachusetts

GPS Information:
N 41°57.849', W071°02.005'

Site Information:
There may be more than one way into this area as there are surrounding streets. The eastern side of Hockomock Swamp abuts the northern part of Lake Nip.

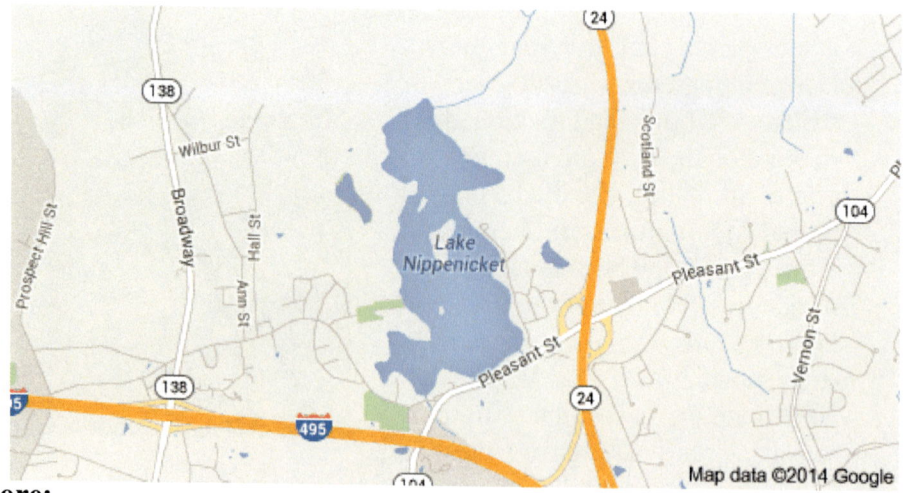

Lore:
Phantom footsteps and shapes dancing around a bonfire are just two of the incidents that have been witnessed at this site along with blue balls of light and snake-like animals watching from within the lake.

Hockomock Swamp

Location:
Route 138, Raynham, Massachusetts just south of route 106 and north of the Raynham Park

GPS Information:
N 41°59.862', W071°04.054'

Site Information:
Hockomock Swamp stretches to both sides of route 138 and there is no formal marking. Look for the high tension wires and you'll know you've found the entrance. This area is heavily used by hunters during deer season so watch for signs or check for deer hunting season announcements. You don't want to become part of the local lore of this area. Parking on the side of the road is permitted; just make sure your car is off the road. There are pathways and berms that lead through the area.

Lore:
The swamp was named Hockomock in Wampanoag which means, "the place where the spirits dwell." Native American burial land is

located in this area. In 1978, Joe DeAndrade witnessed what could have been a Big Foot. UFO's have been spotted several times in the swamp, some even before airplanes in the sky were commonplace. Some believe that the swamp contains a vortex, a portal between dimensions of other worlds.

Tillinghast Hall, Bridgewataer State University

Location: Corner of School Street and Summer Street, Bridgewater, Massachusetts

GPS Information: N 41°59.231', W071°58.373'

Lore:
Bridgewater State University started in 1820 as Bridgewater Normal School, a school for educating teachers. Tillinghast Hall started as a women's dormitory. The dormitories had house mothers that looked after the students in their care. The story is that there still is one housemother looking after her girls throughout the halls in Tillinghast.

Bibliography/References

Dighton Rock State Park

1. http://www.paranormal-encyclopedia.com/b/bridgewater-triangle/, August 29, 2014.

Freetown – Fall River State Forest

1. Balzano, Christopher. <u>Dark Woods: Cults, Crime and Paranormal in the Freetown State Forest</u>. Atglen, PA, Schiffer Publishing LTD. 2008. Print.

Red headed hitchhiker

1. http://what-when-how.com/haunted-places/the-redheaded-hitchhiker-of-route-44-rehoboth-massachusetts-haunted-place/, August 29, 2014.
2. Spooky Southcoast Podcast, "October 27: Annual Bridgewater Triangle Investigation Show". October 28, 2012.

Rehoboth Village Cemetery

1. "Rehoboth author researches local ghost tales", http://www.tauntongazette.com/article/20121028/News/310289913, Taunton Gazette, October 28, 2012.

Shad Factory Mill/Pond

1. http://www.strangeusa.com/ViewLocation.aspx?id=5014&Description=_Shad_Factory_Mill/Pond__Rehoboth__Ma, August 29, 2012.

2. "The Ghosts Next Door", http://www.thesunchronicle.com/news/the-ghosts-next-door/article_ba2de69b-992a-53de-ae95-649b2a9d785a.html. The Sun Chronicle. October 31, 2009.
3.

Anawan Rock

1. "The Capture of Old Chief Anawan", http://www.heritage-history.com/?c=read&author=sabin&book=frontier&story=annawan, August 29, 2014.
2. Anawan Rock, http://en.wikipedia.org/wiki/Anawan_Rock. August 29, 2014.
3. Sentry Paranormal Investigations. http://www.sentry-paranormal.com/blog/2012/08/30/Anawan-Rock-Route-44-in-Rehoboth-MA-and-Freetown-State-ForestHaunted.aspx. August 29, 2014.

Horbine School

1. Emails exchanged with David Dow, Septmeber/October, 2009.
2. The Horbine School: Rehoboth's One Room School House, http://www.strangeusa.com/Viewlocation.aspx?id=5055. August 30, 2014.
3. Legend Tripping: The Haunts of Taunton and Rehoboth, http://www.thebridgewatertriangle.com/2010_01_31_archive.html. August 30, 2014.

Taunton State Hospital

1. Taunton State Hospital, http://en.wikipedia.org/wiki/Taunton_State_Hospital. August 29, 2014.
2. Haunted Locations, http://grandrapidspararnomalinvestigation.blogspot.com/2012/01/037-taunton-state-hospital.html. August 29, 2014.

Mount Pleasant Cemetery

1. Southcoast Ghost: Investigating the Paranormal in Southeast Massachusetts, http://southcoastghost.weebly.com/taunton.html. August 30, 2014.
2. Rhonda Marvel, August 30, 2014

Paul A. Dever School/Camp Myles Standish

1. Southcoast Ghost: Investigating the Paranormal in Southeast Massachusetts, http://southcoastghost.weebly.com/taunton.html. August 30, 2014.
2. Strange USA, http://www.strangeusa.com/Viewlocation.aspx?id=5055. August 30, 2014.

Mayflower Hill Cemetery

1. Pearl E. French. http://www.findagrave.com/cgi-bin/fg.cgi?page=gr&GRid=49460840. August 29, 2014.

Lake Nippenicket

1. Map of Lake Nippenicket, https://www.google.com/maps/preview?ie=UTF-8&fb=1&gl=us&sll=41.9688303,-71.0393766&sspn=6.2963795,11.3074206&q=Lake+Nippenicket&ei=1VEBVNmbNdDHggSEqoLgBg&ved=0CB8Q8gEwAA. August 30, 2014.
2. Nip Story by Marc Svirtunas and Bridgewater Triangle Witness Reports, http://www.cellarwalls.com/ufo/nipstory.htm. August 30, 2014.

Hockomock Swamp

1. The Bridgewater Triangle, http://www.paranormal-encyclopedia.com/b/bridgewater-triangle/. August 29, 2014.
2. Tales from the Swamp, http://www.boston.com/news/local/articles/2005/10/30/tales_from_the_swamp/?page=full, The Boston Globe, October 30, 2005. August 29, 2014.
3. Spooky Southcoast Podcast, "October 27: Annual Bridgewater Triangle Investigation Show". October 28, 2012.

Tillinghast Hall

1. The Ghosts of Bridgewater State University, http://rccblog.com/2010/10/27/ghostsofbsu-2/. August 30, 2014

Thank you Rhonda Marvel!!!

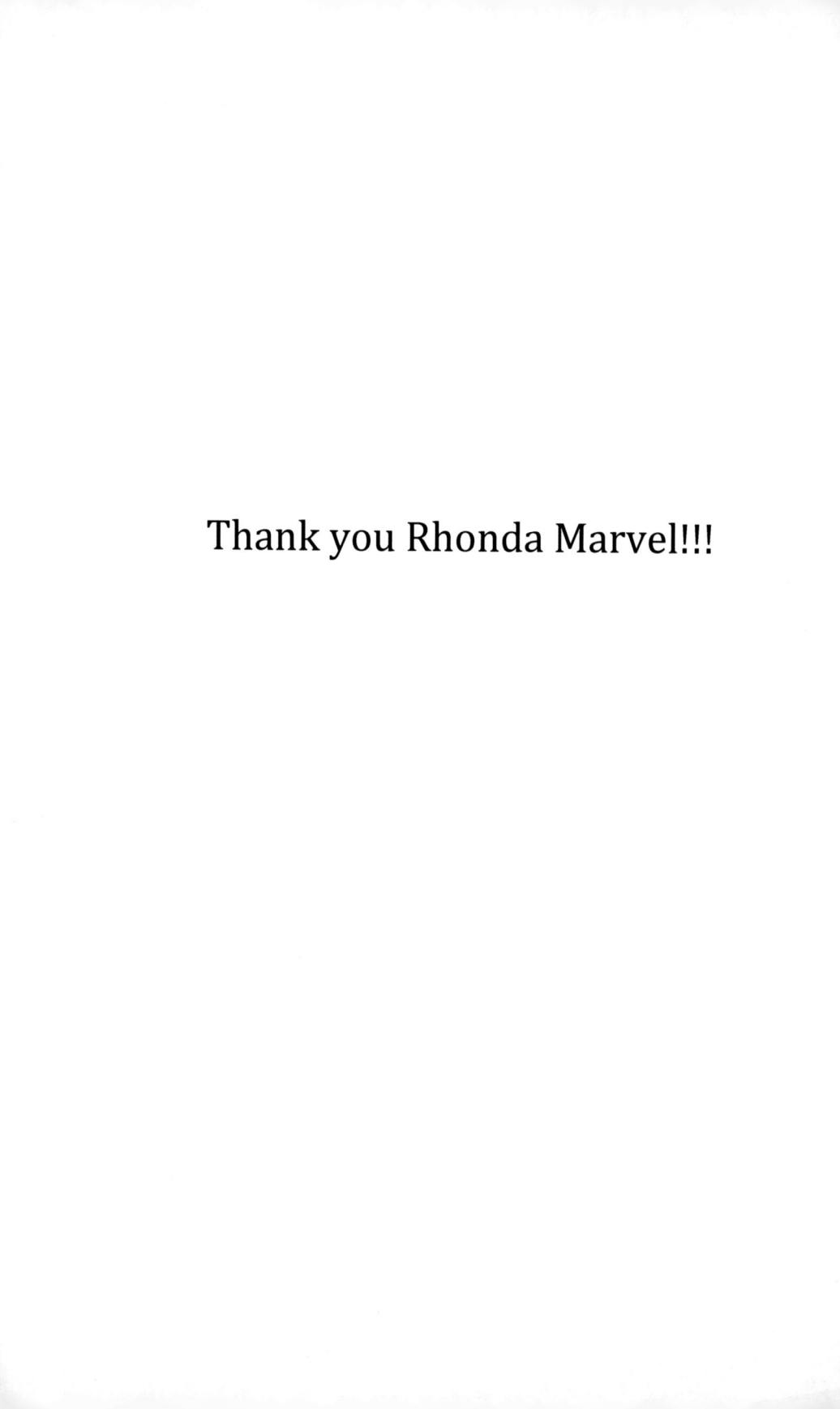

Notes:

Made in the USA
Las Vegas, NV
01 December 2023